this

Cit

d

Being Angry

© Aladdin Books Ltd 2008

Designed and produced by
Aladdin Books Ltd
PO Box 53987
London SW15 2SF

First published in 2008
in Great Britain
by Franklin Watts
338 Euston Road
London NW1 3BH

Franklin Watts Australia
Level 17/207 Kent Street
Sydney NSW 2000

Franklin Watts is a division of Hachette Children's Books, an Hachette Livre UK company.
www.hachettelivre.co.uk

ISBN 978 0 7496 7501 1

A catalogue record for
this book is available
from the British Library.

Illustrator: Christopher O'Neill

The author, Julie Johnson, is a PSHE consultant and trainer, a leading provider of
parenting workshops in London and a child, adolescent and family counsellor.

Dewey Classification:
152.4'7

Being Angry

Julie Johnson

Aladdin/Watts

London • Sydney

Contents

Introduction

These children live on the same street. They are good friends. They all know what it is like to feel angry or what it is like when others get angry with them. Join them and other children as they share their feelings about being angry and how they deal with it.

What Is Anger?

Anger is a feeling which can last a short time or a long time. It can make you behave in different ways. Omar has been feeling cross all day because the day before his friend Jack borrowed his favourite computer game but forgot to ask. Omar felt so angry he shouted at Jack and made him cry.

You may break something in anger.

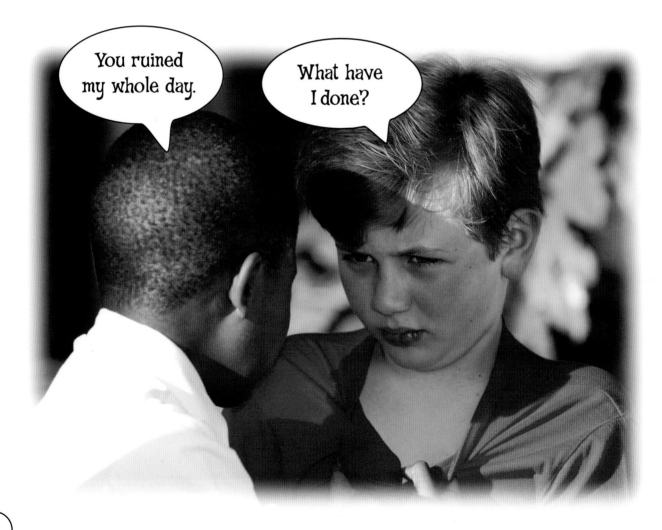

You ruined my whole day.

What have I done?

6

▶ Anger Is A Feeling

Anger is a feeling, like fear or sadness. If you are having a good day and something happens to make you angry, the anger may disappear quickly. If lots of things have upset you the anger may last for a long time. It can rumble away inside you, waiting to burst out.

◀ It Can Be Sudden

People get angry about all sorts of things and for lots of different reasons. Their anger may burst out suddenly, without any warning. Anger can make people say or do mean things.

Omar, what does being angry mean to you?
"Being angry is when you are so cross you say mean things. It can make you want to break something or hurt someone. Being angry can make you want to cry with crossness because you don't know what else to do."

Being Angry With People

Brooke and Naomi are best friends, but they have had an argument. They are so angry that they aren't speaking to each other. Can you remember when you last got angry with someone? Who were you angry with? Can you remember what you were angry about?

You may get angry at school…

…or you may get angry at home.

I don't ever want to speak to Naomi.

I'm not going to speak to Brooke again.

You can't go round to Sam's today.

▶ Why Not?

There will be times when a teacher or parent won't allow you to do something. Sulking, shouting or crashing around won't change their mind. Try to explain why you feel angry. Give them time to explain their reasons.

Oh, I took that book to school.

◀ Brothers And Sisters

If you have a brother or sister, do you get angry with him or her? Perhaps he or she borrowed something without asking? Try to explain how you feel – although your brother or sister may not listen to you. If you feel very angry, talk to your parents.

▶ Best Friends

Even your best friends can make you angry. It may be something they do or say. You may see things differently from one another. You may say, or even do, something unkind. That will only make the situation worse. It won't make you feel better.

I can't wait to play with Paulo.

Story: Being Let Down

1 Simon was waiting for Paulo to come round.

I'm going round to Jake's.

2 Simon rang to find out where Paulo was.

I'm fed up!

3 Paulo had arranged to do something else. Simon threw down his toy in anger.

Why was Simon angry?

Paulo let Simon down. He didn't even say sorry. Simon's feelings were hurt. Instead of breaking his toy, it would have been better if Simon had told Paulo how he felt. Then Paulo may have realised how thoughtless he had been. Simon could have talked to his dad about how upset he felt.

▶ It's All Her Fault!

When someone has let you down, it can make you feel very angry. You may want to shout at the person you are cross with. But being angry won't change the situation. Try to remember that the person may be feeling bad anyway.

◀ It Was A Mistake!

Some people get angry very easily, when there is not much to be angry about. Without thinking, they may hit out with words, or even physically, at someone who they think has wronged them. If you do this, it is important to say sorry.

Brooke is angry because...

"I told Naomi a secret and she told someone else. That wasn't fair."

Naomi is angry because...

"I didn't think Brooke would mind. Then I got angry because Brooke said some really mean things to me."

Being Angry With Yourself

In the playground, Evie is talking to Harvey who was sent out of class for losing his temper and hitting another pupil. Harvey got angry because he was having difficulty reading a book. Have you ever got angry with yourself? Did you take your angry feelings out on yourself or out on someone else?

I hate myself for getting that wrong.

It's not fair. I get angry because everyone else can spell.

But it's not fair to take it out on someone else.

Story: Losing Your Patience

1 Sabrina was building a matchstick model of a house for her school project.

2 She was finding one piece really hard to fix in place.

3 Sabrina became so angry that she knocked the model over and spoilt it.

Why was Sabrina angry?

Sabrina had been enjoying building the house. When she came to a tricky bit she lost her patience because she couldn't do it. She became frustrated and angry. By getting angry with herself, rather than asking for some help, she stopped enjoying what she was doing. She ruined what she had been doing well up to that point.

▶ I Can't Do It!

You may get cross if you are trying to learn a new skill and find it quite difficult. You may get impatient and frustrated and want to give up. Try to remember that it takes a while to get the hang of new things. Practice makes perfect!

▼ Why Did I Say That?

Sometimes people say hurtful things without thinking. They don't always realise that what they are saying is hurtful or unkind. When they think about it later, they may feel angry with themselves for having been thoughtless.

Why was I so mean to my best friend?

Harvey, why did you hit out?

"I got so cross because I couldn't read. Being cross with myself made me cross with everyone else. I didn't think and I just hit another boy. It was really unfair because he hadn't done anything to upset me. I can't always stop feeling angry, but I can stop doing or saying hurtful things."

Angry Feelings

This morning, Ren got so angry he hit his little brother, Kaito. He realises he shouldn't have done this. He has hurt his brother and his mum is now angry with him. It's important not to hit out at people, however angry you feel. It will make the situation worse – and it won't make you feel any better.

Anger can make you feel out of control.

I lost my temper and just hit out.

Anger can make you upset.

▶ Angry And Upset

Anger can lead to lots of other feelings. You may feel frightened by your anger or it can make you feel lonely. You may feel miserable and upset because you don't understand or know what to do with your angry feelings.

▼ Angry And Lonely

Some people seem to be angry all the time. They take their anger out on friends. It may be that they haven't learnt to control their anger.

Friends may put up with this for a while, but may soon choose other friends.

Don't let Dan play because he gets cross if he loses.

Ren, how do you feel now?

"I was wrong to hit my brother, but I wasn't wrong to feel angry. I should have told my mum how angry I felt instead of hitting Kaito. Everyone feels angry, but it's what you do with your anger that can make all the problems."

Hiding Other Feelings

Sometimes anger can hide different feelings. Shelly got angry because she was embarrassed and cross that she couldn't use a computer like her friends. Later her mum explained that some of us just take longer than others to learn to do something. Have you ever got angry to hide other feelings?

Anger can hide a feeling of embarrassment.

I'm getting angry but really I just feel stupid.

Why is she so annoyed? She should just ask me to help her.

Story: Being Bullied

1 Adam was being bullied by a gang.

2 It made him angry towards his family and towards his good friends.

Oh, shut up. What do you know anyhow?

Adam's being bullied at school.

3 Adam's best friend decided to tell Adam's mum what was going on.

Why was Adam feeling angry?

Adam was being bullied. He was frightened, confused and upset. Getting angry with the people he loved covered up these feelings. It would have been better if Adam had told his parents or a teacher about the bullying. They would have been able to help.

▶ A Big Change

If you have to move home, leaving behind your friends and the place that you know, it can make you angry because you are unhappy with all the changes. But once you get used to your new home, you will probably find you don't feel so angry.

◀ Problems At Home

You may feel left out if a new baby arrives or you may feel confused if your parents are separating or divorcing. These feelings can make you angry. It can help to talk to a grown-up, although it may not make the situation change.

▶ That Doesn't Feel OK

If someone touches you and it doesn't feel right, or if they try to make you do something you know is wrong, you may feel angry. You may feel angry if someone asks you to keep a secret which you are not happy about. If this happens, it is important to talk to a grown-up who you trust.

Yasmin, do you get angry easily?

"I only recently came to this part of the country with my family. It meant lots of changes. People teased me at school because of my accent. That made me angry. I was scared by all the new things that were happening. That made me angry, too."

Paige's mum gets angry with her when Paige doesn't tidy her room. Mason says his dad never used to lose his temper, but since he lost his job and is stuck at home all day, he always seems angry. Can you remember who was last angry with you and why?

You may not know why someone is angry... or you may know very well.

Mum gets cross because she says my room looks messy.

My dad is always in a bad and angry mood.

▶ Angry Grown-ups

Grown-ups may get cross with you because you have been naughty or have disobeyed them. Perhaps they have had a bad day at work, are not happy, or maybe someone is angry with them. Grown-ups may take their anger out on someone else, just like you can.

◀ Saying Sorry

If a friend is angry with you because you have let him or her down, why not say sorry? If you don't understand why a friend is angry with you, try to talk about it. Sometimes it helps to ask a grown-up to help you both talk together.

Paige, what do you do when your mum is angry with you?

"If it's because I've been naughty, I say sorry and try not to do it again. If Mum gets angry because she's tired or worried, I try not to get upset by it. If I feel fed up about it, I talk to my grandma."

Dealing With Anger

Omar talked to his mum about why he was angry with Jack. Omar drew a picture of how angry and upset he felt. The next time they saw each other they were able to talk about why they were angry and upset. Now, they have made up.

Try writing down how you feel.

I'm so glad we're friends again.

I'm sorry I was so angry.

▶ Put It On Paper

Try to remember that it's when you let anger get out of control that the problems start. You can't stop feeling angry, but you can take time to think about why you may be feeling angry. Try to write down how you feel – or paint an angry picture!

◀ Ask For Help

If you have had a very bad argument with a friend that you can't sort out, why not ask your parents to help? If you are worried about how angry you feel, talk to a grown-up you trust. Ask him or her what they do when they get angry.

These are Omar and Jack's tips for ways to deal with anger.
"Think before you do or say anything. Think about what is making you angry. Explain calmly how you feel. Punch a pillow or take a deep breath. Try not to take your anger out on others. If you do, be prepared to say sorry."

Don't Forget...

1

How is your reading, Harvey?

"Now that I don't get so angry it's a bit easier. It's still hard not to blow up, but I try to count to ten before I try a difficult word again. You can't stop angry feelings, but you can stop yourself from being unkind or hurtful to other people. It's important to talk to someone about what is making you angry."

2

What do you do when your mum is angry, Paige?

"Sometimes it makes me angry that she is angry with me, when I haven't even done anything wrong! Then I tell my grandma how I feel and that helps me to understand that my mum still loves me – even when she's cross."

3

Do you still get angry with your little brother, Ren?

"I'm going to work out how to share some of my things with my younger brother, but I'm going to make sure he can't reach things which I really don't want him to borrow."

4

How do you cope with anger, Omar?

"Anger is a very strong feeling. It can come on you very quickly. But you can learn to use it and be in control of it. It's not always easy and it takes time to learn. Sometimes I go to my room and shout very loudly or punch a soft pillow. That makes me feel better!"

Find Out More About Dealing With Anger

Helpful Addresses and Phone Numbers

Talking about problems or worries can really help. If you can't talk to someone close to you, then try ringing one of these organisations:

Childline
Tel: 0800 1111
A 24-hour free helpline for children. The number won't show up on a telephone bill if you ring them.

NSPCC (National Society for the Prevention of Cruelty to Children)
Tel: 0808 800 500
Asian helpline: 0800 096 7719
A 24-hour free helpline offering counselling and practical advice for young people.

Supportline
Tel: 020 8554 9004
Email: info@supportline.org.uk
Offers support to children and parents by telephone, email and post.

Parentline Plus
Tel: 0808 800 2222
A 24-hour free helpline offering counselling and support to parents on many issues, including how to help your children deal with angry feelings.

Kids Helpline, Australia
Tel: 1800 55 1800
A 24-hour free helpline for children. Also online help: www.kidshelp.com.au

On the Web

These websites are also helpful. You can get in touch with some of them using email:

www.kidshealth.org

www.nspcc.org.uk

www.childcarelink.org.uk

www.supportline.org.uk

www.parentlineplus.org.uk

www.kidshelp.com.au

www.parentlink.act.gov.au

Further Reading

If you want to read more about dealing with anger, try:

Choices and Decisions: Violent Feelings by Pete Sanders and Steve Myers (Aladdin/Watts)

Thoughts and Feelings: Feeling Jealous by Sarah Levete (Aladdin/Watts)

How To Take The Grrr Out Of Anger by Elizabeth Verdick and Marjorie Lisovskis (Free Spirit Publishing)

Don't Rant And Rave On Wednesdays!: The Children's Anger-Control Book by Adolph J. Moser (Landmark Editions)

What To Do If You Are Scared Or Worried by James J. Crist (Free Spirit Publishing)

Index

Photocredits

All photos from istockphoto.com except 14, 17, 19, 29 top – DAJ; 24, 25, 28

bottom – Photodisc. All the photos in this book have been posed by models.